Silent Reflections of a Fragile Heart

Amy Roullier

Silent Reflections of a Fragile Heart

First Edition: December 2024.
Book Cover via canva.com
Illustrations by ©Victoria Rusyn via canva.com
ISBN 978-1-0369-0642-9 (print)
Published by Roullier Venture Publishing
www.amyroullier.com

"All the most powerful emotions come from chaos - fear, anger, love - especially love. Love is chaos itself. Think about it! Love makes no sense. It shakes you up and spins you around. And then, eventually, it falls apart."

— *Kirsten Miller, The Eternal Ones*

Preface

I have liked and loved in what feels like every way imaginable. I've fallen hard, and sometimes not at all. I've loved unconditionally, and I've loved because I felt I had to. I've liked people simply because they liked me, and I've liked others who only saw me as a friend. I've loved with the innocence of youth, and with the wisdom that comes with age. Loved for their beauty, for the way they made me laugh, or simply for who they were in quiet moments of conversation.

I've liked because I was lonely, and I've loved for the same reason. I've been broken, and I've broken others. I've been unfaithful and have had my trust betrayed. I've liked softly and loved recklessly. Loved slowly, liked quickly. There have been times when I've seen the world only through their eyes, and times when I demanded they make my world their own.

Some were just a fleeting fancy, a spark never meant to turn into a flame. Others were all-consuming—a fire of passion that scorched my heart. Some were reckless, unwise, yet ventured into despite the dangers. Others were gentle and safe, nurturing, and exactly what my fragile heart needed. Some were cruel, dishonest, built on lies and betrayal, while others offered healing, love, and a safety net for my soul.

I've hoped for love to bloom from mere liking, and waited, heart in hand, for someone to choose me. I've changed myself to fit into someone else's world, and I've also stood firm, refusing to alter a single part of me. I've agonized over a message that never came, ignored calls, and ghosted people into oblivion.

I have liked and loved in every shade, from light to dark and all the hues in between. And through it all, I've learned that love is both a thing of beauty and a source of pain—wondrous yet agonizing, graceful yet torturous. It cannot be defined by simple terms or categories. It's neither black nor white but exists in a spectrum of endless grey.

Love, like all powerful emotions, thrives in chaos. It defies reason and expectation. For those of us with fragile hearts, like mine, it's a journey that requires careful steps.

This is a collection of my silent reflections, my unsaid thoughts—now given voice.

Amy

Contents

Hopeful Beginnings

Call me a romantic,
though I'm not even sure love truly exists.

Still, I hope—
that love is out there,
waiting to be found,
and that when it arrives,
it will have been worth the wait.

I want to be found, to be stumbled upon in a crowded room,
where eyes meet and linger, unwilling to look away.
Where nights unfold in endless conversation,
words for the sake of words, exploring every detail.

I want to be carefully unraveled, mind, body, and soul,
each piece laid bare, fully seen and wholly accepted.
I want someone who isn't entranced by idealized perfection,
but finds beauty in my flaws, considers me imperfectly
perfect.

I want to be slowly unlocked, my truths laid open,
my burdens unearthed. Someone unafraid to dive deeper,
to discover all that I am and all I may become—
someone willing to share the weight when it's too heavy,
to stand in every joyous memory, in every moment yet to
come.

I want someone who wouldn't change a thing,
who wants to know every thread of my life—
each joyful recollection, each sorrowful shadow.

I want to be discovered, fully seen and accepted,
loved and cherished, as all the pieces finally come together.

Steady,
my head whispers to my heart,
but the message never lands.
For my heart has dreams
that fly too high,
far beyond the reach of reason.
It craves to run wild,
impulsive,
carried on the wings of eager wishes,
wanting to love without thought,
without measure.
Logic, here, is a stranger—
it would be like shrinking a room
when my heart longs to roam,
open and unguarded,
free from the weight of care,
unburdened by doubt.

Steady,
my head whispers again,
but the words scatter.
And so, instead,
my head says,
I'll stay with you.

I will love you with everything I am—
boldly, fiercely,
because I don't know how to love any other way.
I won't love you blindly.
I see your flaws and quirks,
and I choose to love them
as they are,
simply, wholly.

My love is deep, intentional,
it burns with purpose and passion,
knowing no limits.
My heart only knows how to love
fully and without hesitation,
wild and unrestrained,
without thought for the pain
that loving you might bring.

Because we aren't meant to love cautiously,
or hold back.
We're meant to love completely,
with abandon—
to pour everything we are into it.
If love isn't everything,
then it is nothing at all.

I wish I didn't think of you
at 3 a.m.,
when sleep should claim me,
or at 10 a.m.,
when work calls for focus,
at 6 p.m.,
when friends seek my thoughts,
or at 10 p.m.,
when my mind should be relaxing.

But I'm too excited to sleep through the nights,
too consumed by the hopefulness of us
to enjoy anything else about the days.
I long for other things
to occupy my mind,
but it seems you've already etched yourself
into the quietest corners,
a constant pull I can't escape.

So I'll think of you,
until there's nothing left of me.

If only you were real, not just an illusion.
If only you were here, not just a shadow in my mind.
I imagine you somewhere—not an ethereal vision but flesh and warmth,
someone I could touch, who feels woven into my thoughts,
awaiting that single day we might cross paths,
like metal drawn to a buried treasure, waiting for discovery.
I wish these weren't only hopes and fragile dreams, but truth.
I wish you were here, now, not some distant possibility.
How cruel love is, to let me picture you so vividly,
to shape every detail of who you might be,
and then leave me with only these daydreams—
the outline of you, but never the reality.

When I was younger,
love was grand gestures—
romantic proposals,
public declarations, meant to be seen
and admired.
It was bold,
showy,
impossible to overlook
and demanded attention.

Now, with age, love whispers in small details
behind closed doors:
a long hug after a tough day,
homemade soup on sick days,
a hand resting on yours as you watch TV,
a kiss and a smile at the threshold.
It seeks no validation.
It thrives in quiet, gentle moments
where you and they can truly appreciate its warmth.

When someone is right for you,
everything falls into place—
no confusion, just clarity.
It's as instinctive as loving mushrooms
or hating spiders.
Feelings are simple, easy to understand.
It's us who weave the complications.

I dream of a love that is slow,
intentional, vulnerable and honest.
A love that pushes me to be better,
not just for us, but for myself first.

I dream of reciprocal love—
not where one heart bears more,
but where effort meets effort.
A love without scorekeeping,
where resentments dissolve before they take root,
balanced in both giving and receiving.

I dream of a love that defies the ordinary,
not laden with tradition's weight and expectations' grip.
A love that lives beyond any societal script,
a love that moves in rhythm with my soul.
To be fully seen and wholly respected,
to be supported and yet free to be me—
to trust without fear of heartache,
without the worry that vulnerability
will one day be used as a weapon against me.

I don't seek marriage,
or the conventional forms of forever.
I want the promise that we will love each other
only as long as we truly choose to,
each day, choosing one another anew.

I dream of a love unpossessive,
uncontrolling—a love rooted in empathy,
in the choice to love and to stay.
A love that allows us both the room
to become who we're meant to be,
to chase the things that set us alight,
and to return, time and again, to one another—
to find home in each other after wandering.

I want a love that expands my world.
A love that understands:
for love to thrive, it cannot be all.

This is the love I dream of,
a love that makes space, that stands strong
yet free, one that breathes life outward,
rather than turning our worlds inward and small.

Before you fall, do you know their intentions?
Do you know if they want you as deeply as you want them,
if they'll fall with you, or if you'll fall alone?

Before you fall, do you know them?
Do you know what they look like on a bad day,
as well as on their best?
Will they care for you when you're sick,
stand by you when you need them most?

Before you fall, do you know what they're capable of?
Will they choose kindness when cruelty tempts,
will they be gentle when the world is not?

Before you fall, do you know their past as intimately as their present?
Are their stories honest or written from your hope?
Are they open, or only as transparent as they need to be?

Before you fall, do you know if your heart is at risk?
Is their love a game of manipulation, or pure and steady?
Is it safe to fall?

Before you fall, do you trust that you'll be your own protector?
Can you trust that you'll walk away if you must,
if your choice turns out wrong?
Do you fall because you want to, not because you *need* to?
Before you fall, are you certain you can catch yourself?

It is so important
that you don't settle
for any relationship.
I promise
it's worth waiting
for the right one.

When I fall in love,
I misjudge its fragility,
as delicate as a flower.
Too much shade, and its petals wilt;
water too often, and it drowns
before it has a chance to bloom.
A flower can weather a storm,
but hail and thunder
will eventually strip it bare,
reduce it to nothing.
I am never careful enough with love,
creating conditions
where the flower must fight
just to survive.

You say I can stop fighting against you
and start fighting with you.
Yet every moment together feels like an offense,
because I've fought alone for so long
I've forgotten how to stand alongside someone
who's on my team.
The instinct to defend is hard to shake,
but I yearn to learn this new way.

How is it that you can meet someone so seemingly perfect,
yet feel no trace of that magic spark?
Why does that small glimmer,
that fleeting twinkle, mean so much?

It's a mystery—the way perfection alone
can't conjure the warmth, the pulse,
the quiet electricity that says,
"Yes, this is it."

No one tells you how to stop running
when it's all you've ever known.
You run from dark places,
from those who hurt you,
from broken relationships,
but you've run for so long,
that even safe places bring no comfort.
Your feet itch,
restless, uneasy with stillness,
aching for the familiar rhythm
of foot meeting ground.

So, you keep running,
from good places,
from those who love you,
from relationships that matter,
until you've forgotten what you're running from.

You keep chasing an invisible finish line,
hoping that one day,
you'll cross it,
and trust someone enough
when they say,
"You can stop now. You're safe here."

I’ve learned love can be a storm gathering strength,
a seed waiting to burst through the soil in spring,
the quiet shoreline of a distant island,
or a bridge trembling under the weight of crossing.
It breathes life into a weary soul,
and shatters a heart in the blink of an eye.

Bold and daring,
quiet and meek.
Steady as a river,
as predestined as the next volcanic eruption.
Love feels like red wine on a winter’s evening,
or sand sneaking into your sandwich.

Love is not one thing or another;
it is ever-changing.
The way we love,
how we receive and give,
it is constantly in motion.

Love is not the same for you
as it is for me.
It is never the same each time we love.
How can we ask love to bend to our rules,
when love creates its own?

Your Hand in Mine

I was lost and broken,
pain echoing in every corner of me,
yet you swept me up,
silencing the storm with your quiet presence.

You held my hand
as I pieced myself back together,
bit by bit.
Some fragments you helped me find,
while others were mine alone to carry.

You told me it was okay
to have lost my way,
to still be searching for pieces of myself.
You loved me through the brokenness,
just as much as you would when I was whole.

The puzzle lay in pieces,
but you saw the picture it could become.

There was no hard or fast fall for us,
no rush, no frenzy.
We had all the time in the world
to fall slowly, deliberately.
You said, 'Let's be friends first,'
and so we were:
friends who supported each other,
near or far, through rough times and smooth.
Good friends stick together, you said.
Then you said, 'Lean in,'
so I leaned—
gently, carefully, over time.
I leaned in, and you didn't step back;
you held steady, embracing me.
You said, 'Trust me,'
and so I trusted—
cautiously, with a hint of trepidation.
As time passed, my trust took root,
and you met it with trust of your own.
You said, 'Let's be soulmates—
not two halves seeking to be whole,
but two complete lives, choosing to walk together.'
And so I chose you, and you chose me.

The only true relationship
is one where you lift each other up,
where you both grow
into more of who you are,
and more of who you're meant to be.

My definition of love used to be this:
Love meant giving everything.
Losing yourself completely and willingly.
Love was sacrifice.
If you die, we die together.
Love was a fairytale where nothing else mattered
as long as we kept the flame alive.
Love meant compromise of self—
letting go of all other connections, pouring everything into just one.

Love was never calm, never stable.
It was lightning, fire, and chaos.
Unpredictable, volatile, burning so brightly that
being scorched every now and then felt inevitable.
Love meant being so entwined
that I couldn't see where I ended, and you began.
If you fell off a cliff, I'd leap after you—
because anything less wasn't love enough.

Love was intense and uncontrollable,
a surge of feelings and fire.
An unstoppable force submerging me in its embrace
as if I had no choice but to drown in its waves.

Love meant two people drowning together,
even when one was pushing the other down
just to stay afloat.

But today, my definition of love has changed.

Love is warm, steady, a slow burn.
It's holding hands, but not giving up your life.
Love is championing someone's passions
while they champion yours.
It's giving without losing yourself in the process.

Love is respect, balance, and boundaries.
It's having difficult conversations
with someone you're willing to do the work with.
Love is acceptance—of yourself and your partner.
It's honesty, vulnerability, kindness—without judgement.

Love is staying when the fun fades,
when the dishes pile up, and you're both exhausted,
too tired to speak.

Love is being apart but trusting completely.
Love means continuing your own growth
and cheering your partner on as they do the same.
Love is calm, resilient, but not without effort.

Love is putting on your own life jacket,
and then offering to help with theirs.

You say it’s okay to be vulnerable,
but I don’t know how to tear down these walls.
Brick by brick, they’ve kept me safe,
protecting me for so long.
I fear dismantling this fortress
might disrupt everything within.
What if I open up, only for you to leave?
I’m not sure I have the strength to rebuild.
If I did, I would raise those walls higher,
ensuring no one could breach them again.

Six years of living alone,
about to say goodbye to this solo life
I thought I'd be eager to leave behind.
But now, as it teeters on the edge of *ours* instead of *mine*,
I find myself holding tight to everything I've loved about my own space.

The simple pleasures—
spreading across the whole bed,
dinner whenever I choose,
furniture picked solely for me.
The peace and calm of a place that's fully yours,
spending time however you wish.

Soon, my solo life will end.
I didn't foresee how it would feel
to make room for someone else.
Even when you love them, even when they feel right,
there's a quiet grief I hadn't anticipated,
a finality to a way of life I've come to love.

I took it all for granted, didn't cherish it enough.
Now there's so little time left to savor these moments,
this sanctuary of singularity before it becomes *ours*.

We talk about the transition from togetherness to solitude,
the challenge of regaining self after a partnership,
but I can tell you this—
returning to shared life, to *we* after cherishing *me*,
is a complexity all its own, one rarely spoken of.

I say it boldly:
"I want you, but I do not need you."
Yet beneath the words,
I fear my want
might betray me—
that what I call desire
is, in truth,
a quiet, aching need.

Love me or Leave me

Perhaps I choose unwisely,
or maybe love chooses me,
foolishly.
For we disappoint one another,
again and again,
always trying
to make the other bend
to our will,
only to break
beneath the weight
of our own expectations.

There’s a big difference between a slow burn
and minimal effort.
A slow burn still shows up—it’s steady, comfortable,
a warmth you feel is on the right track.
If they like you, you’ll know.
It won’t be hard to figure out or a mystery to solve.
The signs will be clear.

A person who cares will have a steady determination.
They’ll show up, make real effort,
and work to win you over, again and again.
Not occasionally, not just when it’s convenient.
They’ll want to spend time with you, learn more about you,
see you—
consistently and sincerely, even if it takes time.

Minimal effort, on the other hand, is constant confusion,
just enough to keep you wondering,
just enough to keep you invested,
but never enough to stop the doubt,
never enough to stop you questioning everything about it.

I’m used to being
the one before
true love arrives—
a stepping stone
on the path they walk.
I heal their wounds
while they carve new ones into me,
deeper each time,
until my weary heart aches with the weight
of being the one not chosen.
Her loves are always in motion,
always heading onwards,
upward,
never pausing to see
the love waiting quietly inside me.

Perhaps I was meant to be muse,
inspiring her future lovers,
a whisper in their love stories,
never a place to settle,
just a shadow to pass through.

So use me as you will,
fading lover,
for I have little left to give,
all my longing saved
for the next one,
and the next,
and the next.

Love me or leave me—
don’t let me linger in uncertainty,
wondering how it will end.
Will we be a tale of two souls
destined to unite,
or a hopeless tragedy unfolding?
Clarity is all I seek,
for the in-between is a heavy weight.

What if you are my person,
the one I'm meant to spend a lifetime with.
What if you are a slow burn,
and with patience, will you blaze brighter?
What if you're just shy, guarding your heart
until you feel safe to show its full warmth?
What if this is our story, just beginning?

But what if you're nothing?
Not a page, a chapter, or even a footnote in my novel?
What if you're just a smudge on the page,
a mark that should have been wiped clean,
a distraction that mars the sentence?
What if you're only a passing moment,
a scene not worth the time it's taken,
one best discarded and forgotten?

They say the right love finds you
when you least expect it.
But it's been years
since I expected anything from love,
and still, it hasn't appeared,
not even to catch me off guard.

I’m one foot out, neither here nor there,
ready to walk away but not prepared to walk within.
An eye on the door, not quite looking, not quite hoping,
just poised to leave at a moment’s notice.

I wait for you to make the first move—
I won’t jump in together, just in case this is a play,
just in case this isn’t forever.
So here I am, hovering by the edge,
watching what you do without giving anything away,
letting your thoughts linger, while mine stay tucked away.

I like this sense of control,
believing I’m one step ahead of you.
But really, I’m stuck, rooted in the same question:
what should I do?

Eventually, a choice will have to be made—
to leap or to step back, to be outside or within.
But for now, I’ll stay where I’m most comfortable,

with one foot out, neither out nor in.

I fight a battle
when the other side
hasn't waged war against me.

I bring the drama,
when I despise chaos,
and I yearn for peace.

I see the problem—
in Taylor Swift's words,
"Hi, I'm the problem, it's me!"
Yet I haven't found the solution.

I’ve spent more time uncomfortable in relationships than at peace.

Why stay, you might ask.
Perhaps I never learned what healthy love looks like.
Maybe I self-sabotage,
as it’s all I’ve ever known.
What if I run toward chaos,
breathing in the disarray,
because focusing on our discomfort
lets me avoid the ache within myself?

It’s better to be alone
than with someone
who makes you *feel* alone.

Shoes scattered beside the rack,
a growing pile of clothes by the bed,
socks abandoned on the floor, waiting
as if they might learn to wash themselves.

Tools stray outside the garage,
litter lurks beside the bin,
half-full water glasses stack on the nightstand,
a washing load idles in the machine,
waiting for someone else to move them.

Nearly empty jars, the last drop of milk,
cupboards drained which cannot replenish themselves.
The last banana. The last curl of butter. There is no more
pasta.

The sink always full.
The house now a walk-in wardrobe,
walking through the dining room a hazardous affair.
And when she trips, she wonders which stray thing will be at
fault.

These things may seem small, as if they don't matter,
as if she doesn't mind. But she does.

She minds because she is not your parent,
your keeper, your maid. She minds
because her free hours are ground down
to another load of laundry, another stack of dishes.

She minds because she wanted a teammate,
not an opponent.
She minds because these small things
chip away at her softness, slowly,
day by day.

I loved you for all the wrong reasons.
I was lonely,
craving someone to fill the emptiness within.
You poured your love into my hollow spaces,
and so I loved you, because it was you
who softened the ache of solitude.
I loved you without meaning to.
I never intended for us to be love,
to get this far.
We were meant to be casual, fleeting—
a brief romance after the long, hard end
of the one before.
I loved you because I feared being alone again.
I loved you to fill my thoughts,
to avoid facing myself.
I loved you selfishly,
in ways that weren't right, for reasons that weren't fair—
a love born of gratitude:
you loved me, so I loved you back.
You loved me purely, in the right way—
not out of need or obligation,
but simply because your love existed.
I loved you because I needed healing,
needed proof that I could still be loved.
But in mending my broken heart,
did I break yours?

You promised rest in your arms,
free of burden and worry.
"Don't worry, darling," you said,
"Let me help you carry the weight."
No need to fight for us,
or take the lead.
I believed in your strength,
that together we would thrive,
our love blooming effortlessly.

At last, I thought,
someone to rely upon,
equal teammates,
someone to trust,
to allow my gentleness space to unfold.
For I've longed to be tender,
to love softly,
rather than take charge.

But time has unraveled your words,
revealed them as echoes of intention—
empty promises,
my burdens unchanged.
Once more, I find myself the leader,
the weight heavier,
moving forward,
dragging you along in my wake.

Don’t be an “if I get time”
Be an “I’ll make the time” kind of partner—
Or one day,
You’ll wonder why they let go
of someone
they never really had.

I’ve stayed with the unsure,
held on to the doesn't know,
clung to the wants me for now
but avoids the talk of tomorrow.
I’ve lost sleep wondering how to be more,
do more, give more of myself.

I’ve agonized over people,
countless hours spent in my head,
waiting for them to be ready,
while they thought of me
no more than a passing breeze.

If I could offer just one piece of advice:
Save yourself the days, the months,
and eventually, the years
spent waiting for feelings to grow
in places they never will.

Listen to your instincts—they are not your enemy.
They’re telling you this isn’t enough,
you deserve more,
and they are not the one.

Love yourself enough to walk away
from someone who isn’t all in.
Love yourself enough
to save yourself.

Love them
for what they do,
not for what they promise
to do someday.
Intentions may inspire love,
but it thrives
only through action.

I don’t know if it’s fear that keeps you distant—
fear of being hurt,
of vulnerability,
of letting me in.
Or if your love
is simply lukewarm.

What I do know
is how hard it is
to connect with someone
who loves from afar,
who holds me at arm’s length,
unwilling to truly know me.
You’re content to stoke the fire
just enough to keep the embers alive,
but never enough
to let it catch into flames.

I keep trying,
and I’m not sure why.
Maybe I’ve convinced myself
that lukewarm might be enough.
But I know better.
Lukewarm love leaves me cold,
confused,
restless—
reaching for warmth
you’re not willing to give.

If you bend yourself to please them,
you’ll never find peace in pleasing yourself.
And one day, when you finally want to be seen
as whom you truly are—
if they haven’t loved you without the mask,
it’s unlikely
they’ll stay for what’s underneath.

There’s nothing wrong with knowing what you want
and standing firm to find a relationship that aligns.
If others choose to lower their standards, so be it.
Every relationship involves compromise, yes—
but let’s stop implying that someone’s needs
are something they should compromise on.

You, your time, your presence, the love you offer—
they hold value. Know your worth,
because you deserve only great things.

When you finally figure it out—
comfortable in your own skin—
rejection feels inevitable,
acceptable
and somehow,
welcome.
Because if they can’t embrace all of you,
and you’ve found peace in *who you are*,
you're content to let that fish swim away
or toss the catch back into the sea yourself.

It took me a long time to unlearn
that being careful with whom I share my life
isn't being too picky or hard to please.
It's honouring the value of my time,
knowing that the person I choose
can make those moments feel full, bright and pleasant,
or merely tolerable at best.

Modern Dating:
The Untamed Beast

What a peculiar game we play—
I, the mouse, you, the cat.
You toy with me for a while,
until boredom creeps in.
You hint at my escape,
dangling me on a string,
teasing hope with your touch.
What keeps you coming back?
Is it mere boredom?
Do you need a mouse to play with,
a spark to ignite your thrill?

You claim your love will flow freely
once you've explored my body,
no need for inquisitive words,
our skin will speak
the language of hearts and minds.
But in the quiet stillness,
as I lie beside you—
not in your arms—
I feel your curiosity already fading.
Touch has not sparked
what words always do:
the emotional tether.
Now, we are two bodies
who know each other deeply in flesh,
but not at all in soul.

This one could be the one that changes everything.
No marks, no stains, only light tones—fresh and untarnished,
a blank canvas tinged with vibrant potential,
awaiting its first, tender brush strokes.

It could be dark, fierce sweeps of black and grey,
but you hope this canvas will find its way
to the strange beauty of surrealism,
a place where unconscious dreams are made real.

There's so much excitement for what might come next,
a feverish thrill at what you two could create together.
Every first moment—your first date, first kiss,
the first time they fall asleep beside you,
the first morning you wake together—
each is a treasure, a memory in the making,
each an imprint on your heart.

With each touch, your wonder grows,
your anticipation deepens, filling you
like a well of possibility. Yet,
without noticing, you create a chasm.
You stand at the cliff's edge,
casting hopes and dreams into the void below,
believing it will fill, never realizing
the chasm only expands—
the ground growing ever distant,
receding just out of reach.

Then, suddenly, you fall.
Were you pushed, or did you trip?
Does it even matter?
False hopes had kept you teetering at the edge,
convinced the chasm was a safe place for your dreams.
But it was not safe. It held only empty promises
and illusions of what could have been,
lifting you up only to cut you on the way down.

Each unfulfilled promise now sharp,
a reminder of the depth of deception.

It isn't the time you lost that breaks you.
It's the shattering of hopes,
the dreams for a future that almost was,
that leaves you in pieces.

After years of casual, fleeting connections,
unintentional and uncommitted,
I find myself longing for something
with meaning and purpose.
Yet, I can't bring myself to trust
that it won't just be another disappointment
dressed as something real.

Let’s be soulmates for a day,
fake lovers for a single night.
Let’s pretend we’re destined,
as fate plays its hand.
Let’s bare our souls,
talk until the stars grow tired.
Let’s find comfort in our alikeness,
declare our shared flaws
insignificant against the fire between us.
Undeterred by the world outside,
we’ll stoke the resting embers in our hearts,
and set our spirits ablaze.
But just for today—
because why settle for one love
when countless kindred spirits
promise something new,
a different kind of true?

Do you know what hurts the most?
That love seems destined
to slip through my fingers,
never staying longer than a fleeting dream.
It whispers of home,
a refuge, safe and warm.
It tells of commitment,
a bond unyielding.
But love deceives me,
over and over.

Online dating is an untamed beast—
wild, unpredictable, emotionally unavailable.
The possibility of a real connection
feels more distant than ever.

People treat people like objects,
disposable, rejectable,
"Not real" enough to deserve respect.
Mistreatment is rife,
an ecosystem that thrives on disregard,
tearing at your mental health,
chipping away at your self-worth.

It promises no guarantee of love,
And only guarantees a heap of problems
you never wanted, and never needed.

I’ve tried again and again
to be the perfect person
for someone else—
to meet their wants, their needs,
often before my own.
For a time, I lost myself
in the pursuit of connection,
putting them first,
myself last.
I forgot to ask,
What do I want?
What do I need?
Do they align with my hopes?
Do they reflect my dreams?
I spent so much energy
trying to win them over,
I never paused to ask:
Are they the right one
for me?

They don't make love
like they used to,
when it spanned eternity
rather than filling moments.

This line is murky, hard to read—
between someone who might grow to reciprocate feelings
and someone with no intention of transforming this into
something more,
content with neither commitment nor progression,
happy to string me along for their own comfort and reward.

But I am done with hypothetical romances,
the endless guessing, month in, month out.
Keep your lukewarm tokens of affection,
your hollow declarations.
Don't bring me anything wrapped in shallow intent.

I may sometimes confuse a quest for love
with a need to manage loneliness—
but I know what I feel,
and I trust what I know.

A situationship is no longer my situation.

Love goes far beyond appearances.
If someone can't cherish your heart,
your quirks, your essence,
the beauty of your imperfections,
then looks will never hold enough weight.

You'll tire yourself out
chasing an unattainable ideal,
a battle against time,
because age is relentless;
our beauty will fade.

But your inner self,
the facets shaped beneath the surface,
remain unwavering.
They compose your soul,
the truest part of you.

Seek love that longs to connect
with the depths of who you are.

I think back to all the love letters
I wrote in high school,
when liking and loving felt the same—
words spilling out of me, desperate to find their way.
Fear of rejection didn't hold
my thoughts captive.
I wrote with boldness, saying everything
all at once, letters scribbled in the reckless rush
of a heart unafraid.
As if time might run out,
and my truth had to be told,
or I would drown in the silence.

Now, my love letters have turned into texts,
and fear grips my fingers.
Too afraid to write the words I carry,
too cautious to send what lingers on the screen.
"Text too much, too fast, and they'll lose interest," they say.
So I'm no longer bold,
no longer desperate to be heard.
More often, I say nothing at all,
as if speaking might extinguish the flame—
and it feels safer to disappear into the quiet
than to voice what lies within.

Your name was your first lie,
one of many yet to unfold.
Then came your age—
your face told truths your words withheld.
You dazzled me with accents,
pretending you were from afar.
I fell for the charm,
not seeing the fraud beneath the rouge.
How blind I must have been
to miss the layers you'd draped so carefully.
How desperate, to be fooled
by a penniless guitar player's fantasy.
You weren't one, of course,
that was simply your style—
witty, flirty, and thrilling,
doing anything for a smile.
You sought my adoration,
and I gave it far too freely.
Ignored your evasions,
tried not to seem too needy.
In the end, everything about you was false,
you held no truth, no integrity.
You hid behind the mask you'd crafted,
incapable of genuine honesty.
Sometimes we pass each other on the street,
and I wonder if you're real now—
I wonder who you are beneath it all,
and realize, I'll never know.

Our bodies spoke the same language,
but our hearts dreamed different dreams.
I sought love,
you sought another conquest.
My hopes drowned out my instincts,
which whispered that your touch deceived—
it promised desire, whispered commitment,
but only played a game.

I longed for commitment,
offering my body as a home,
a place for you to rest in.
I mistook your fleeting pleasure
for something deeper,
as if passion could stand in for affection.

But you desired inconsistency,
to remain untethered,
never too close to anyone.
Your actions betrayed your true motive—
to satisfy a hunger
that could never be fulfilled.

Once upon a time, I believed in second chances.
If someone sought redemption
with genuine intention,
to face their flaws and begin again,
I thought maybe they deserved forgiveness.

But sometimes people only want absolution,
not to heal,
but to keep their grip on control.
If you forgive them, it feels like permission,
and if you permit it,
you hand them the power to repeat their wrongs.
And often, they do,
simply because they know they can.

They don't seek a chance to do better,
just a chance to test the limits of your compassion.
It's not about change;
it's about curiosity—
can they still cross the line and be welcomed back?
Can your forgiveness heal
what a lifetime of habits won't?

Maybe, deep down, they hope too,
which is why they return to the scene of the crime.
Maybe they dream of cleansing their conscience,
of starting over.
But their resolve is fleeting,
and whether they mean to or not,
they fall into the same patterns.

Fool me once, because my heart is forgiving.
But you won't fool me twice.
My compassion may be boundless,
but it's also merciless
when it sees the truth.
And I'll cut you loose

without a second thought.

I don’t fear the end—
pessimism has proven me right,
again and again,
that endings are inevitable.
How can you then fear
what you always expect?
But what I do fear
is trusting someone who feels different,
letting doubt slip through just enough
to go all in,
only to face the pain
of being proven wrong,
once more.

This Might Destroy You

And I wonder:
is love broken,
or am I?

In the past,
I glorified self-sacrifice
in the name of *love*.
What mattered to me
became secondary
to what mattered to my partner.
Their wants, their needs—
always came first.
Because my relationship with myself
was fractured,
I sought worth and acceptance
in theirs.
And in doing so,
I made their happiness
more important than my own.

One day you,
will meet someone
who shows you everything love ought never to be.
And when you part,
the way you love
and the way you want to be loved
will be forever changed.

I like weird people—
odd ducks, eccentrics, loners,
those who huddle in corners,
hidden away from the crowd.

I like the ones who need unravelling,
who are complex, sometimes unsettling.
Give me a challenge,
because if it's too easy, I'll get bored,
and find another odd duck to amuse me.

I'm drawn to those too confident,
as if they hold a secret the world has missed.
I like the ones you know won't end well—
the fire that burns too bright and hot,
yet something about the flames
makes you reach for them anyway.

I like the ones no one notices,
the ones discarded as unworthy.
I like to believe I saw something others couldn't,
even though, more often than not,
there's nothing much to see at all.

I like the ones that keep you guessing,
who maintain emotional distance.
They toy with your feelings,
come close, pull away, come close again—
treat you kindly, then with cruelty.
I'll stay, waiting for the person I first met
to reappear from behind the mask.

I like the ones who treat love as a game,
always needing to win.
Hook me in with love bombs, affection,
and I'll be yours,
even when the mask falls

and the monster beneath emerges.
I'll believe I can fix you,
like Beauty saving the Beast.

I like the liars, the cheaters.
Lie to me, and I'll believe it.
Treat me unkindly, then say you love me,
and I'll accept it.
Shower me with devotion,
then betray me, and I'll forgive.

I like the ones who want to be chased,
who give little but expect much—
who starve me of affection,
withhold their kisses,
send messages that trickle in slowly,
leaving me days without reply.
I'll keep my calendar open for you,
waiting for the next meeting that may never come.
I'll fight for scraps,
craving your validation so desperately
that I'll never want to leave.

I like the ones who consume me,
who demand my time, my attention,
who let me lose myself in them,
knowing I'm slipping away but never minding.
I like the ones who destroy carefully, slowly,
with intent or with carelessness.

I like the ones I shouldn't stay with,
the ones I should walk away from.
I like to believe I can turn this wreckage
into a fairytale,
even if it's built from ash and dust.

You can love someone
and want them in your life,
but sometimes,
even then,
they're not meant
to be part of your story.

I shouldn’t give you all of me
when you offer nothing in return.

I shouldn’t hold this relationship up,
when you're determined
to tear it down.

Don't ask me to surrender everything,
to sacrifice myself just to keep us alive.
For I will suffocate myself
to hold onto this dream,
while you turn every moment into a nightmare.

Let's not talk. Let's not reach across this silence.
Let's weaponize it, tiptoe around each other
like landmines.
Let's be awkward, angry,
wrapped in unspoken words
until someone finally gives in.
I'm angry.
You're angry.
What started this fight? I can't remember.
Who's wrong? It doesn't matter.
Now, it's just about who will break first.
Is this love?
I'm not sure.
But this is love for us:
indignant and irritated,
days of hateful silence,
weeks of tense resignation.
It doesn't feel like love,
but it has become ours—
tainted, broken, heated, outraged.
Not what I thought love would be,
yet here we are,
loving each other in this vexed quiet,
holding on through the friction.
Maybe silence is best,
or maybe it's just best for us—
a reprieve when the quarrel subsides,
a fleeting calm in the eye of the storm,
where unease stews quietly,
peace mingles with dread of the next clash.
Perhaps I want the silence to stretch as long as it can—
a respite before the battle resumes,
when the unspoken words echo louder than sound
I can avoid the question that haunts me:
is this what love is meant to be?

A toxic relationship is never a safe space.
Staying in one risks losing pieces
of who we are.

Hopeful, foolish, naïve—
I didn't know love could be dangerous.
I didn't know what I didn't know
until you taught me:

Love can be an anxious knot,
tight in my stomach,
words stuck in my throat
for fear they'd come out wrong.

Tiptoeing through daylight,
eggshells beneath my feet,
not soft sand as I once believed.

The edge of a storm,
cold winds rising,
dark clouds swelling,
thunder cracking closer and closer—
nothing like the warmth of sunshine
or the sweet scent of honeysuckle.

No birdsong, no peaceful shade
beneath the trees
where I once thought love
might always be.

I lost my voice for a time.
I would speak,
but my words went unheard,
and so I grew quieter
and quieter,
until I forgot I had a voice,
and they forgot I was there.

I stayed when they treated me badly,
stayed where I was not valued,
stayed while they chipped away at everything I was,
hoping to destroy everything I had been
and could be.

I convinced myself it was better to be with you
than without.
I excused your cruelty,
swallowed my pain,
and buried the truth when my lies became
too loud to ignore.

I couldn't face it:
that I had made a mistake,
chosen unwisely,
read you all wrong.

I stayed long past reason,
ignoring the signs, hoping for change,
hoping we could go back,
rewrite the beginning,
start again and become what we once were.

I left only when the stone in my shoe
grew into a rock that stopped me in my tracks.
Only then did I see my own worth,
realizing self-acceptance could lift me
where you had dragged me down.

I left, wondering if I could be enough on my own,
knowing I deserved better,
hoping I could be better for me.

But it took so long to leave.
I dressed you up like a fairytale,

clung to the story of you,
instead of the truth.
There were two of me:
the one who had to survive,
and the one pretending not to.

For almost a decade, I lost the best parts of myself,
spiralling in a place that offered no peace.
Now, I am left searching for fragments,
pieces to mend, putting myself back together,
one by one.

My life is so different from the one I imagined,
the life I built but had to escape.
I've been lost so long,
I'm not sure I have the strength to find myself,
to build a new beginning.

But then, I remember—
I didn't know my own power
until I found the courage
to walk away from you.

When you rely on someone else
to tell you your worth,
it's all too easy to depend on their words.
And when you lean on them
to lift you up,
it's all too easy for them to tear you down,
to destroy you, if they choose.

Self-validation—
the ultimate act of compassion,
of empathy, of care.
It's not easy, nor simple,
to cultivate these things within yourself,
to learn that your voice
should matter more than anyone else's.

But it is essential.
Only you should have the power
to lift yourself up—
or tear yourself down.

Some people bring out the worst in you—
they drain your energy,
make you feel small.
They argue endlessly,
never listening, never letting you speak.
One sided conversations.
You feel unappreciated,
disrespected,
unsupported,
misunderstood.
“Why do you put up with it?” they ask.
But it’s hard to explain
something you don’t understand yourself.
Your loyalty is unwavering,
but sometimes, loyalty
comes at a cost.
And the price?
Your own well-being.
Oblivious, or maybe not,
you cling to history,
as if it could ever outweigh the present.

I stare into the mirror,
but I don't recognize the reflection.
"Who are you?" I ask.
"I am you," they reply.
How strange to not recognize this face.
that tells a story of pain etched over time.
So very tired, so very lost.
How did this become us? I wonder.

People who love one another
don't stand idly by
while the other sinks;
they dive in,
ready to pull you back to shore.

We tell ourselves that love is all that matters—
but it isn’t.
When love can be toxic,
frightening,
maddening,
abusive.
Love alone
should never be enough.
And often, what we think is love
isn’t love at all.
In those moments,
the healthiest choice you can make
is to walk away from someone you love.

It’s worth being the villain in your story.
The story you’ve shared with family, friends,
anyone who’ll listen.
The one where I left you suddenly, without cause
or warning,
where I am the bad guy who hurt you beyond words—
but not so far beyond that you can’t recount
your edited version of why we ended,
why we’re now finished, finite, no more.

It’s worth being the villain in your story.
The one where you cast me as a monster,
tear down my character, drag my name through the mud.
I used to hate that people might only hear your 'truth,'
but I’ve learned to embrace my role
as the villain in your story
if it means I can be the hero in mine.

It’s worth being the villain in your story.
For the peace I’ve found outside its pages,
the calm, the quiet, the rediscovery of parts of myself
I once thought were lost.

It’s worth being the villain in your story
because it means, finally,
I’m free to create my own.

I loved you unconditionally, without strings,
without expectations.
My love flowed with the hope of your happiness,
with hope for your success, a quiet cheer in the background,
selfless and unassuming.

I loved with kindness, with compassion, with empathy.
I loved you the way I longed to be loved: openly, wholly,
accepted.

For ten years, I loved unconditionally,
standing by you at any personal cost,
even when I shouldn't have—long after it began to hurt.

You loved me conditionally,
your love an impossible puzzle of rules and restrictions.
One wrong step and it was gone, a game where I danced
like a puppet on a string for her master, lifted in your
approval, discarded in your displeasure.

Your love was unpredictable, unreachable,
demanding ever more for each inch given.
Your love thrived on power, and in that power, I became
small.
I became powerless for loving you.

Your love wasn't love; it was control,
built on my fear of your reactions,
on what might happen if I failed to please,
if I stepped out of the lines you'd drawn.

Your love wasn't love; it was slow suffocation
of something pure. I'll never understand
why my love needed tearing down, destroying,
to dismantle, to diminish.

I see now: my unconditional love was no match
for your conditional boundaries. We were opposites—
a free spirit against a cage.
And a free spirit must either be released,
or eventually, she'll die.

I didn't want to spend my life shackled in your prison,
a cage I'd mistaken for love. I didn't want to wither,
until all that remained was an echo of me.

A free spirit remembers, eventually, her courage,
her strength.
She holds peace, serenity, and resilience at her core.

You mistook my softness for weakness. But I was only soft
until I found the courage to break free,
to step beyond your walls and reclaim a life unshackled,
untamed, unchained.

And in that moment, I remembered:
the unconditional love I'd given you belonged, always,
to me.

When your heart aches to be noticed,
and your soul longs for connection,
we must choose wisely who we let in.
For the fierce desire to be loved
can drive us to seek intimacy
in the shadows of the wrong places.
Let us guard our hearts,
for true connection blooms in the light.

Endings

Beneath it all,
I feel you slipping away.
Your heart has already moved on,
no longer mine,
while mine lingers, grasping at hope.

I hope for you
in every message,
each ring of the phone,
hidden in corners of places
we once claimed as our own.

Another day fades,
but still, I hope.

I hope for you
in strangers' beds,
within the arms of new lovers,
body after body,
trying to resurrect a story
only we once knew.

Time slips away,
but still, I hope.

I hope for you
to remember the way we laughed at dusk,
how we wandered through dawns,
fingers entwined, hearts brimming.

We once believed our love was destined to be endless,
perhaps my memory distorts the past
where we no longer exist.

I hope for you to return,
but the distance now is too great,
and too much time has passed.
Still, I hope.

They forgot me long ago,
while I waited,
lingering in the same spaces—
the ones we once called ours.
Hoping, always hoping,
that one day they might return.

My heart stands on fragile ground,
held together by careful hands,
so delicately mended
that one more fall
could scatter the pieces
beyond any hope of repair.

They say distance
makes the heart grow fonder,
so we chased our dreams separately.
But the solitude carved a chasm between us,
and our dislike grew more visible.
Our closeness slipped over the edge,
into the blackness,
taking our connection—
our hopes, our dreams for a life together—
with it.

Distance has not strengthened our love;
it has weakened it,
slowly dissolving
as if it were never there.

We keep returning home,
hoping love is waiting,
hoping it has grown
in the days we were apart,
still believing that separate lives
might create a beautiful life together.

But love is no longer waiting.
It has moved on,
a leaf chasing the wind.

Again and again,
I walk away,
only when secured
in another's arms.
Guilt gnaws at my insides,
but solitude looms larger,
a shadow I cannot bear,
darker than the weight of my own betrayal.
I fear solitude
more than the self-loathing
that festers within,
the ache of the hurt I've caused you.

When I walked away from you,
I left a piece of myself behind.
So small, I thought I wouldn't miss it.
But as time passes,
I realize it might have been
one of the best parts of me.

I sense that our time is slipping away,
that the end of us is close.
You've changed in the smallest ways:
your touch has grown distant,
your affection feels worn thin.
No longer do you look at me with warmth;
your gaze is weighted with the decision I know is coming.
I could ask you to stay,
but I won't beg.
I could ask what changed,
but you won't say.
I could ask how to make us whole again,
but some part of us has shifted,
something beyond repair.
I only wish I knew what it was.
Why our love withered and died,
why what once felt endless
has turned so brief.
I wish you didn't have to go,
but it seems inevitable
that you must.

When someone rejects you—
and they will, because rejection finds us all—
remember, it's not as personal as I know it feels.
We can't love everyone. We don't even like everyone.

It doesn't mean no-one will ever love you,
or that you aren't loveable.
It just means you weren't meant for them,
as much as they weren't meant for you.
And that's okay.

Rejection saves you from time wasted,
time better spent elsewhere.
Rejection is a gift, because your time is precious—
too precious to give to anyone
who isn't 100% certain
that you're right for them.

You might be reaching out for forgiveness.
You might be testing the waters,
wondering if I could forgive enough
to let you back in.
But I am empowered by the act of no action,
the choice to let you pass by
without any need to understand
what you want this time.
No part of me feels compelled
to explore why you've returned.
There are no regret here, only gratitude
that something ended which was never right.
I'm thankful for the lesson learned.
There is no need for apologies,
for repentance or closure.
I healed on my own;
nothing further is required from you.
Seek your closure elsewhere.
There's no need for conversation.
Time doesn't haunt me with 'what ifs'—
it fills me with reflection,
without the illusion that we were,
or could have been, anything more.
It offers only the truth:
two people who didn't fit together.
You are a part of my past, not my future.
If you're looking for forgiveness, I forgive you.
But I do not want you back.

We've been here so many times before,
when words poured out in desperation,
pleading with one another to find a way
to make it work.
When our hopes and dreams
still clung to the edges of possibility,
when we cared enough to fight
and loved enough to hold on.
And yet now we sit together in silence.
Words fail to right the wrongs;
no expression can soothe the wounds.
There are no more hopes,
no more dreams,
no unsaid words left to voice.
We have spoken it all,
and still, it remains unfulfilled.
There is nothing left to say.

I’m sorry I let you go.
I’m sorry I didn’t try.
I’m sorry I let fear take over.
I’m sorry I convinced myself you didn’t like me,
and that I didn’t like you either.

In the quiet of late nights,
I find myself scrolling through your social media,
and something aches,
perhaps a wrong that can’t be made right.
I’m sorry I have too much pride to reach out,
to admit I might have made a mistake.
I’m sorry you’ve moved on—
sorry that you did it without me.

I regret not being brave enough to take the risk,
for never giving us a chance.
You linger in my mind as a regret,
when I once vowed never to regret anything.
But I regret us.
I regret that I didn’t fight for what we could have been.

I’m sorry that I miss us.

I didn't see this coming—how wrong could I be?
To have woven a fantasy so heavy on a falsehood that you were meant for me.

Did you not say you loved me, that you'd never before felt this way?
If that was true, then why is there this steep and terrible price to pay?

There was you, and then there was nothing.
There was you, until there was no more.
You can't love me, you said, not in the way you once swore.

It was all a daydream, a fleeting fairytale at best,
a brief and hopeful mirage, but together we failed the test.

I am broken and in darkness, with you went all my light.
But is this how we end? Am I meant to fight?
Should I beg you to reconsider? —yet that would be in vain,
for you can't love me as I need, and I must accept the pain.

I cry until there are no tears left, nothing left for you and me.
I mourn what we might have been, and all we'll never be.
I drift through days like a ghost, my mind a foggy mess.
I've never felt so hopeless or under such distress.

Could you not have taken this pain with you? Or not inflicted it upon me at all?
Once you made me feel taller, but now I'm so very small.

My heart aches with a noise, a thunderous, deafening tear.
Where once my heart felt whole with us, it's now shattered beyond repair.
Where once I thought our life assured, it's now a life we'll never share.

They say that something better will come, but I don’t believe there’s better than you.
They say that love will heal, but I don’t see my heart mending anew.
There are cracks that no time will repair, tears that won’t ever heal,
not with patience or someone else—some wounds will never conceal.

You’ve left an everlasting mark, one I can’t let go,
even if, in the end, I was merely a string to your bow.
I will find a way to move forward, I will bear this pain and survive,
but don’t ask me to forget us, or to dream that one day I’ll thrive.

For that day will still be missing a presence, a part of me I once knew—
two halves of a whole, two pieces of one.
That person will always be you.

Maybe time will heal nothing.
Maybe it will heal everything.
Maybe time will pass,
and still, nothing will make sense.
For time is just time.
It holds no answers,
only the minutes
to contemplate what they might be.

There was you—and then, nothing.
My everything, now my no more.
How cruel love can be,
to offer a world of possibilities
without ever intending to see them through.
There was light, then only darkness.
My hopes, and the shattering of my dreams.
How unkind love can be,
to show me such wonders, then draw the curtains
on a story that was never meant to last.
Ask me if I would do it all again,
and my answer would be no.
But give it time, for in time, love
may soften from cruel to bittersweet.
One day, I might remember
the joy of loving, of being loved,
and the promise of what could be.
But today is not that day.
Today, I will despise love
and all it has cost me.
Today, love mocks me
for being so open, so idealistic.
Today, love is not my hope or my dream;
today, love is my enemy.

Sometimes,
things don’t work out,
but in time,
understanding blooms.
You’re being guided
toward something greater.
Trust the journey.

I used to be a risk-taker.
I would fall in love without hesitation,
believing love was always worth the cost.
But now, I am careful.
I am cautious and guarded,
because I've learned that love can break you,
unexpectedly,
and my heart, older and wiser,
is so very tired of being pieced back together,
never quite the same as before.
So, when I start to like you too much—
when I feel myself caring more than you do—
I choose our ending.
I choose the pain I can handle,
the hurt I can control.
I know you want me to stay,
to wait and see if you can get to 'more.'
But that means taking all the risks,
risking my heart on unspoken promises,
on the fear that I'll fall completely for you,
and you may not fall for me at all.
I've been there before,
and I won't go there again.
It's easier to let you go,
to leave the 'what could have been' unknown.
To choose self-protection over the gamble of love.
I no longer take risks with my heart.
I am her protector.

It’s time to move on,
to change your life,
to want more for yourself.
It’s time to grow, to evolve—
into what,
you haven’t yet decided.
But it’s time to seek
a new way of living.
One without the pain of the present,
one filled with hope for the future.
It’s time to let go,
to walk away,
to accept the truth
that you cannot stay.
You will be okay.
You will heal, in time.
You won’t always feel broken.
You’ll grieve for what could have been,
for the "us" that never came to be.
But deep down,
you just know—
it’s time.

They always come back
when you've healed and moved on,
just as you've almost forgotten
what you had together,
when the bad times
are clearer than the good.

They return to remind you of the past,
to test your boundaries,
to taunt you with "What if…"
to erase the version of them
you've come to hold,
replacing it with who they wish to be.

They always come back
when you've stopped hoping
for them to knock on your door,
when your gaze no longer lingers in their direction.
They arrive unexpectedly,
catching you off guard,
the chase sweeter now
with a new you to conquer.

And you hate yourself
for the way you feel—
for convincing yourself you've healed,
moved on,
no longer interested.
You remind yourself
that your love was full of holes,
where trust and care
seeped out instead of in.
Yet, a whisper stirs within,
growing louder:
"What if…"

Let’s not do this again.
Let’s not begin,
not fool ourselves
into believing we’re more
than we truly are.
Let’s not blur the lines
between fantasy
and reality.
Let’s not allow loneliness,
a longing to feel wanted,
to disguise what this really is.
Let’s let go of one another,
stop here.
No more messages
after long silences,
no more checking in
under the pretense of care.
Let’s leave this
where it should have always stayed—
in the past.
Let’s say goodbye
or leave the farewells unspoken.
Let’s not do this again,
and again, and again.

You are a part of my past,
not my future.
That means you have no place
in my present.

If I had to heal from you once,
I'm not letting you back into my space.
The person who allowed those mistakes no longer exists.
Your return now only brings disappointment—
disappointment that I let it happen in the past,
that you still think I would,
that you believe I haven't seen through
your self-serving games,
or that I'd accept them again.

This is your lesson, not mine.

Don't message with expectations of a reply.
I am no longer waiting at the other end,
like I used to be.
Because if I had to heal from you once,
I'm absolutely not letting you back in.

You taught me that some people aren't meant for me,
that a breakup is not a rejection, just an ending—
and that every end becomes a new beginning.
In my solitude, I learned to love myself more than I ever had,
more than anyone else ever could.
Your absence has been a gift, and I treasure
knowing my own worth now.

This place I'm in doesn't allow repeats
of what I've already known as painful or toxic.
I will not lower my boundaries for disrespect,
nor adjust my standards to fit your needs.
I refuse to let my healing unravel,
to let you back into my life just to serve your agenda,
one that has nothing to do with me.
I don't deserve that, and I will not tolerate it.

I'm moving forward, not backward.
You are a part of my past, not my future,

and so you have no place in my present.
This is what self-love looks like—
choosing myself, first and always,
without hesitation.
I am normalizing self-respect, because I am worth more
than unreciprocated energy
that will never fulfil me.

I will not hold space for you
when you've never done the same.
I've healed from you once; I won't do it again.
You needing an ego boost, or to feel wanted,
is not my purpose.
My purpose is my own happiness, my own growth.
An ex from the past is not the answer.

So, if I had to heal from you,
I'm absolutely not letting you back in.
I've moved on.
I suggest you do the same.

I remember the day we stood facing each other,
nervously reciting vows we hoped would echo through time.
"Until death do us part," we declared,
but death hasn't claimed us,
and yet, here we are,
each a world apart.

Divorce is the quiet acceptance
that all those hopes and dreams,
the future that once seemed certain,
are no longer yours.
It's okay to mourn—
not just the end of a marriage,
but the loss of the life
you thought you'd have.
For me,
it felt like a death.
I grieved not only for my marriage
but for the future I'd woven so tightly into it.
Coming to terms with the end
meant letting go of the comfort
in believing my path
was already laid out.

This is where I leave you.
No more words to be spoken,
no tears left to shed.
I've circled the endless possibilities,
over and over in my head.

But this is where I leave you,
where we come to an end.
I can't keep up this charade,
a game of pretend.

Pretending we love one another,
faking that we care,
when love left us long ago,
and even like vanished into thin air.

The choice isn't easy,
and it won't be without pain,
but continuing this pretense
makes us both players in a hollow game.

Where once we were kind to each other,
kindness lives here no more.
Our love has grown cruel, spiteful,
and I still don't understand why for.
Why our love couldn't go the distance,
why our souls became so misaligned.
Why love fades after so long,
and yet I still pine for what was mine.

But not at the cost of staying.
I must leave—not just for me,
but for you, too.

We are not our best selves together,
we've lost what was good.
So, I will go, and we must accept the end,

because our days are too few.
Far too short to waste on a dream
that has wilted and died.
When there are other dreams to chase,
those dreams won't include me by your side.

Not all relationships
are meant to last forever.
Sometimes,
relationships shift and change,
ending for no other reason
than you simply outgrew each other.

There isn't just one person you're meant to be with.
There are many with whom you can find connection.
A lifetime holds the capacity to love freely and widely,
without limits or boundaries.
How many you choose to love—
that's entirely up to you.
Love doesn't hinge on fate or a single chance encounter.
It's not something beyond your control.
Love is resonance, connection, and—above all—choice.
The choice to commit,
to stay,
to love each other for as long as that love endures.
You choose your person,
whether for a moment or for a season.
Which means there is no "The One" in the literal sense—
there are endless possibilities.
You choose to love one person
for as long as the love lasts.
And when it ends,
you can love again,
over and over,
as many times as your heart allows.

I Held Everything I Needed

I transformed pieces of myself,
yearning for your gaze,
but your eyes drifted
to distant horizons.

In my quest for your recognition,
I lost sight of who I was.
But then, I turned to the mirror—
there, I found my reflection,
and with it, the warmth
of love, compassion, and kindness.

In that moment, I realized
I had all I ever needed.

I fell in love with my flaws,
forgave my mistakes,
and decided to love myself—
not as a perfect version,
but honestly,
with all the scars and cracks,
and the quiet strength they carry.

I may not be single forever—
I will probably date again,
one day.
But right now,
in this moment,
I am happily single,
falling head over heels
in love with dating myself.
And every time
I think I might be ready
to open my heart to someone new,
I feel an even stronger pull
to keep focusing on myself,
pouring that love
into me.

Watch as I keep myself afloat
when no one knew I was drowning.
See me wrap my arms around
this fragile form
and make it stronger than I ever imagined.

Watch as I transform anger into love,
filling the emptiness with appreciation
for my own complexities.
Watch as I rewrite my story,
starting anew,
with or without you.

Watch as I fall deeper in love
with who I'm becoming,
and with who I have yet to be.
Watch as I learn that my worth
is not defined by others' gaze.

Watch as I give myself another chance
to uncover what I've always needed,
hidden quietly within me.

Sometimes, they call me *brave*
because I walk alone—
out in the world where everyone can see.
So brave, they say,
as if solitude were a secret,
to be kept private,
to be hidden,
wrapped in apology,
shrouded in shame,
never out in the open.
But why is being alone, brave?
I wonder—
are we so afraid,
of facing the quiet echo
of our own company?

It’s both a burden
and a gift
to feel so deeply.
I have loved and loathed
in extremes—
my heart, fragile,
expands and cracks
over and over,
pressed beneath the weight
of emotion.

But ask me if I’d choose
to be numb,
to escape the storm
instead of feeling it all,
and I would choose
to carry this weight,
to feel everything,
deeply.

We are always changing,
dismantling who we were yesterday,
rebuilding who we might become tomorrow.
And so, today becomes
the precise moment in between—
the bridge between who you were
and who you hope to be.

Love is tangible in so many ways.
It's in the message from a family member
just checking in.
A friend calling to catch up,
because they miss the sound of your voice.
In a Facebook tag—
a post that made someone think of you.
Love, lives in the everyday exchanges,
in conversations with colleagues,
in the stranger's smile and quiet "hello"
as you pass by.
It's there when someone reaches out,
asking for help, or offering it when you need it most.
In times of loneliness, hold tight to that love.
We are surrounded—
by people who love, cherish, and care for us,
in ways small and infinite.

We are all searching to be found
in one way or another.
Although I never considered that finding myself
might be the most important way
to be truly discovered.

I’ve loved many people,
but loving myself
has been my greatest joy.

Dear Fragile Heart,

I know your soul is weary, and I'm truly sorry that love has shown you both its beauty and its pain. But I hope you remember that it's okay to unguard your heart and try again. Love defies reason, expectation, and logic. It exists not in absolutes but in a spectrum of endless shades of grey, meaning it's never the same each time we love. The next time you open your heart, a new experience, different and unique, will await you. Don't let past hurts tarnish what the future may bring. Life has room for love in all its forms, without limits or boundaries. And if one love ends, there will be more opportunities to love, as many times as your heart allows.

I hope you realize it's okay to love fiercely, recklessly, without caution. For our hearts long to dance in the flames of passion, even with the risk of being burned to ashes. Allow yourself to love deeply, to dream of a love that's everything you desire and more. The weight of unfulfilled dreams is far heavier than the sting of failure, and it's better to chase the stars than to stay grounded, too afraid to soar.

If love has treated you unkindly, I hope that the next time it will be gentler. I hope this love will understand why you've built walls around your fragile heart and that it will hold you close long enough for you to feel safe enough to let them down. One day, someone will love you with genuine empathy and acceptance, and you will trust them enough to rebuild your foundations on love, not fear.

You've made mistakes, and I hope you can find it in yourself to forgive them. Perfection isn't necessary. This journey is one of many lessons, and the next stage will bring wisdom and a deeper understanding of yourself. It's time to grow, to evolve—into whatever version of yourself you choose. I promise, you will be okay. And in moments when you feel too weak, I hope you'll remember just how powerful and capable you truly are.

You may feel fragile, dear heart, but remember: you have saved yourself time and time again. No matter what lies ahead, you will catch yourself, for you are held together by hands that are powerful, full of warmth and boundless compassion. In your hands, you hold everything you need to face whatever comes your way.

I know you wonder how you can become unbreakable. But maybe we're meant to break, to stumble, to fall, and to shatter into pieces. Because in healing, we grow—into someone wiser, stronger, more resilient. We become something greater. So perhaps sometimes we are meant to break, for something magical unfolds when we piece ourselves back together.

I hope you love again and again—softly, passionately, compassionately, in every possible shade. I hope love finds you in the most unexpected places, hidden from plain view, quietly waiting to be discovered. I hope you encounter a love so fierce it sweeps you off your feet, then laughs with you as you rise together. I hope you see love in a stranger's kindness, in the unwavering trust of friends, in the genuine care someone shows for your well-being. And I hope you find love again and again within yourself, embracing who you are, accepting your imperfections without judgment, and nurturing an unconditional love that fosters inner peace and reminds you of just how lovable you truly are.

About the Author

Amy lives in Lincolnshire. A part-time vegetarian and full-time lover of carbs (her true soulmate), Amy simply cannot function without a morning caffeine fix, which fuels both her creativity and her day-to-day life.

Writing has been her passion since her teenage years, though life took her in a different direction for a while. Four years ago, she found her voice through an online blog that challenged negative stereotypes about being single. As she shared her experiences with mental health struggles, personal losses, and the messy, often misunderstood side of adulthood, she discovered a deeper connection with others facing similar challenges.

Silent Reflections of a Fragile Heart is Amy's debut book, a heartfelt collection of poetry, prose, and personal reflections on love, heartache, and healing.

Printed in Great Britain
by Amazon

54879386R00082